MW00413198

A LIFESTYLE OF LEARNING

Insights for a family considering homeschooling

Copyright © 2019 Vickie Takei
Rock On Living Publications
All rights reserved.
ISBN: 9781796730753

A Lifestyle of Learning
Insights for a Family Considering Homeschooling

Copyright © 2019 Vickie Takei
Rock On Living Publications

ISBN: 9781796730753

Publisher contact information:
Rock On Living Publications
2211 Lakeshore Dr. Raleigh, NC 27604
(919) 609-3834
www.qvtakei@yahoo.com

Printed in the USA

DEDICATION

This contribution is dedicated to every parent, on every continent, in every time.

Your story, despite how insignificant it may feel at times, has, and will, continue to be an integral part in the story of the evolution of the human race.

How we educate our children will determine the course of history and ultimately the survival of our planet.
Truly.

Finally,

To my mother. She left my life at an early age and it has been the single most profound influence on how I live. Her departure cleared a pathway that would not have been possible if she had remained. For that, I am eternally and forever grateful.

Contents

-A NOTE FROM THE AUTHOR-

Hello! I am so glad we have connected!

Please join me on social media to share and collaborate!

IG: @rockonliving

FB: Rockonliving – homeschool

Neglected Blog: www.rockonliving.com

My intention in creating this book was to encourage the family considering homeschooling or making a major change in their life.

Life is short, too short to waste one day not being and doing what makes you feel alive. If you are considering change, I am on your side, cheering you on, friend!

--

A LIFESTYLE OF LEARNING

Insights for a family considering homeschooling

~CHAPTER ONE~
THE JUMP

"Sometimes the people around you won't understand your journey.
They don't need to, it's not for them."
- Joubert Botha

*g*f you are reading this, I am guessing you may be desiring change - something different. That is my hunch. You hear the call late at night whispering *"is this it?"* I know. I was there...

Perhaps it isn't homeschooling, but just a big change, a shake-up in life? On more nights than I can count, I laid in bed going back and forth on withdrawing our girls from public school and bringing them home. I *thought* I was only contemplating a different way of educating our children, but what I have learned, is it was a **different way of living**.

I remember in my late 20's my husband and I went skydiving. Before our jump, we watched a brief safety video. After our "training," I was strapped to the front of a retired Navy Seal and taken 3 miles into the sky in a little propeller plane.

When we reached the altitude to jump, they opened the hatch-door to the plane – they opened the door to the plane – take that in for a second...*they opened the plane door three miles above the earth.*

It was cold, loud, windy and our green and blue marble of a planet looked so far away. The instructor looked at me and yelled, *"You're first!"*

All these years later, I am not lying, my hands still sweat as I recall this experience. We waddled to the door to get into position. I was in the open doorway. My toes were dangling over the transition of the plane. Crouched at the

2

doorway I could see the outside of the plane – I was looking at the wing of the plane, I could touch it. I was standing between the plane (safe) to free-falling (not-safe, but exhilarating.)

I looked back at my husband and I was **T.E.R.R.I.F.I.E.D.** *terrified*. If I had been last in the line of jumpers, I may have chickened out, but everyone was sardined tightly and waiting to jump.

My partner yelled in my ear, *"just rock back on me and then we will roll forward..."* I have never felt more scared in my life.

I trusted and let go...

I jumped.

I shut my eyes for the first 10-12 seconds of our jump...it was too much. It was loud, the wind was strong, and I was falling. I was freefalling to earth. I was not on the plane, I was not on earth. I was freefalling – untethered.

After two miles of free-falling, my instructor touched the top of my head. This was the signal that we were going to open our parachute.

The second we pulled the cord to open the chute, everything changed. It became silent, slow, peaceful, beautiful. This transition from freefalling to opening the parachute is like a hurricane changing over from the tumultuous outer bands to the silence and peace of the storm's eye.

We swirled, like a leaf falling from a tree and I got to see the big picture – *Earth never looked more beautiful.* It was an incredible moment where I saw life differently. I guess you could say, my world-view changed *from* a change in my view.

If you have ever sky-dived before, you know as you approach your landing you experience something called 'ground-rush.' It can be frightening.

After soaring and coasting down to earth, the ground appears to suddenly rush up and if you're not careful can freak you out! We skidded to our landing and my legs were so weak, I could not stand for a moment. But, I did. Changed, forever.

Big changes do that!

Big changes or experiences sometimes require overcoming fear, a leap of faith, disorientation and a re-entry to life. They can leave you with a new life-view - a broadened world-view. I believe these are the moments where you are 'living' and can be the booster shot needed to enjoy other areas of your life, too.

You make a change and it allows you to grow deeper in your understanding of yourself and builds the muscle of courage *to do* life. You grow as a human.

I don't know if this analogy will help settle your mind, but honestly, if you have a desire to be with your family (a lot), learn together and have the courage to try something different, this jump may be for you. Regardless of how much you read, study or prepare, it truly requires a leap of faith.

If you have a desire to be with your family, learn together and have the courage to try something different, this jump may be for you.

I spent many of our first years homeschooling anxious and looking for 'proof' that we were not going to mess our kids up forever. I felt lost at sea for about two years. Disoriented, I found myself repeatedly saying "I feel like I have lost my footing."

Everything was new, foreign and counter-culture. Quinn and I were both public-schooled and up until this point, so were our girls – we knew what that looked like. But, for homeschooling, there was and is no one-size-fits-all blueprint. I found myself trying to explain and put a form to something I didn't quite get myself, yet.

In hindsight, I **had** lost my footing. I was standing in the transition between viewing school as 'other' and something did separately from home life and school coming home and becoming a **lifestyle**.

For about two years, I remember when our family was seriously considering home-schooling, I scoured the internet for books, blogs, and testimony about **how** families came to the decision to homeschool. My kids were in public school and doing well. I needed to hear people's thought processes as to *why* and *how* they brought their kids home and honestly... if it 'worked.'

Quickly, I discovered there wasn't much out there for us-at least families like mine who were not considering home-schooling for faith-based reasons. I discovered there were and are a lot of resources available for that group. While homeschool families owe much debt to these pioneers of home education, this was not our story or *our why*.

As the number of families choosing homeschooling is swelling at record rates, I believe there is a new group or type of homeschooler emerging and *those* were the people we were looking for. We needed help navigating this uncharted territory. We were looking for families who were restless for not only a different way of educating their children but living their lives.

I was looking for families that were happy with their lives... and still wanted more.

I found my inspiration in a book called *Becoming BareNaked* by Jenn Barenaked. Now, before your mind goes to the gutter, as the title does make one go, *"Hmmm..."* stay with me...This book was about a family tired of the status quo. A family of five that had worked hard and achieved *The American Dream*.

6

This family was good, but discontent. They were looking for **more**...more time together to learn, to travel, to grow, **TO**gether as a family. This family left a six-figure income, sold two homes and set out into the unknown with three young children.

They homeschooled. I liked that. But, homeschooling was one small piece of the masterpiece they were creating. Homeschooling was almost a byproduct of the style of life they desired for their family. Education happened, for the most part, *in* the world. This family stepped out of mainstream America and had the courage to do something different. On their terms. And they did it together.

Life is too short to settle.

The book, *Becoming BareNaked* is a raw, collection of Jenn's handwritten notes and is a glimpse into the inner thinking and thought process this mother was going through **before** they made the decision to sell it all and blaze a new path. *It was the book I needed*. It wasn't a homeschooling book per se, but a book about having the **courage to go for life**! To be brave and make decisions that are true to you, even if they are counter-culture.

The name *Becoming BareNaked* is a metaphor for how they are living their life...in the wide open for all to see, no lies or covers. Just their truth.

Becoming BareNaked was our impetus to jump. I provide a list of books at the end of this guide containing some of the resources and books I found helpful on our homeschool journey. I hope they may help you, too.

~CHAPTER TWO~

OUR STORY

"The man who is swimming against the stream
knows the strength of it."
– Woodrow Wilson

Our family falls under the category of the "unexpected homeschoolers." Homeschooling was a foreign concept to us. My husband, nor I, never once, *ever* contemplated or discussed homeschooling in our entire 20-something years sans kids. We went to public school and always just assumed our children would do the same.

About 12 years into the parenting gig, we found ourselves not satisfied. Things were good, heck, in many ways, we were great by many people's definitions. We were living the "American Dream." I became a stay at home mother (once again, unexpected), we had a big house, manicured lawn, three children in several activities and they were succeeding in the public-school paradigm.

I volunteered in our girl's elementary school classrooms and served on the PTA for years. At no fault of the teachers, I witnessed a significant amount of time spent on non-academic matters such as waiting, cleaning, setting up and transporting students to the next activity.

I observed curriculum selected to prepare students to pass a standardized test at the end of the year. Very little student-led or interest-based learning was occurring in the classroom. Therefore, I witnessed many unengaged, uninterested students. Sadly, some of these students were already being inoculated to think they were not 'smart.'

I found the amount of time spent on homework meaningless and intrusive. Too often, there were assignments with little to no significant meaning to our children. Our girls (who were in elementary school) would come home from school close to 4 pm and then, most nights, were asked to complete another 30-60 minutes of homework. Some days, our girls would go straight to their fun activities which would bring them home for dinner and then bed. I felt like we were living a wash-rinse-repeat life and it felt a little lackluster and dull.

I spent hours of my life checking backpacks, returning permission slips, marking checklists, sending in requested items to the teacher and school. I performed teacher assistant jobs (because of lack of staffing.) I felt like I was on a hamster wheel of existence straining my eyes to look for signs of life. I was looking for a life where learning was fun and a natural part of their growth and development.

Our girls had one teacher in second grade that movies are made of – *she was the best* – and other years, not so much. We were entrusting our children's childhood and lifelong relationship to learning to some teachers not invested and burnt-out. I felt very uneasy allowing my child to spend an entire school year in that type of environment. It felt like luck of the draw.

But, these were things I think we could have handled or figured out. I know no system is perfect. I believe these were not the explanation of what was happening to my husband and me – something fundamentally or philosophically was changing at our core.

I remember thinking at one point, I work hard and give many hours of my week to the school and other people's children – what if I focused on giving this to my family and our girls? I felt so conflicted about this because I always felt volunteering at the school was a form of community service that was at the heart of my being and I was invested.

But, something was off - not balanced - we were restless. It wasn't the standardized tests, homework, underfunded/staffed schools, bullying, mass shootings, or the myriad of other reasons - we could have handled all that if we felt our children's unique, individual blueprint was being nurtured. The system, by design, squelches outliers and celebrates conformity and academic ability to take tests well.

I saw several very engaging, bright young children separated and labeled as 'behind' their peers because they were unable to reach certain benchmarks set by the system. A system designed to move massive amounts of kids grade level to grade level at one time.

Labels can be dangerous. Sometimes they become a self-fulfilling prophecy and we become what we are told – especially when we are young and impressionable. Our kids were not receiving the nurturing and guidance we desired. They were spending the best hours of their days doing things that were not moving them closer to their highest potential. And, for us, learning – learning that is interest based and starts with curiosity - was thwarted in school where the focus was to teach to an end of year test.

Homeschooling felt like swimming upstream without a paddle. We didn't realize how indoctrinated we are to send our kids to school, *it's just what you do*. It is easy to abdicate the responsibility for our children's education. IT is easy, it is the norm. This wasn't going to be easy – were we ready and able to accept this accountability?

We felt pressure from the system, some of our friends, family and even strangers. Think about it - if a child fails or messes up in public school, it is easy to point the finger at the system. But, if a homeschooled child fails or messes up, if our kid falls off the tracks, the finger will be pointed at us. That's scary.

We started to ask ourselves big questions:

❖ What values in our home were not being met in school?

❖ Why were we leaving a year (a YEAR!) of education up to a teacher that couldn't be bothered to call or email me us back regarding simple questions or requests?

❖ Why was it ok for the person who was going to have the largest influence on our children's relationship to learning not partner with us as parents?

❖ Why were our children doing homework?

❖ Why were we settling for a system that is in many ways felt like "luck of the draw?"

❖ Why is bullying on the rise? What is going on in our schools and young people's hearts that this

13

is how they are handling their feelings?

❖ Why is anxiety, depression and teen suicide at an all-time high? What is going on in their homes, schools and lives? What has changed?

❖ Why are gun shootings and violence rising in our schools?

❖ How can we allow our kids to sit in a system that is raising and releasing kids that think this type of behavior is normal or should be accepted? **While we work on the answers and solutions as a society, our kids were in the system NOW where there is no do-over.**

❖ How can our family have more quality-time? How do we create less 'to do, check-list' living? How can we transition into more *being* and less *doing*?

❖ How can we better partner our girl's unique personalities and educational needs?

❖ Can we afford to homeschool? Do we have the financial stability and ability to do this? What changes to our lifestyle are we willing and able to make to bring our girls home?

❖ How much of a say do our girls get in this decision?

- ❖ How do you educate three children, three grades?

- ❖ Will our girls resent being homeschooled?

- ❖ Are we going to mess up our kids by removing them from the system or norm of public education?

- ❖ Could we actually educate our children 'better' than public school?

- ❖ Could we redesign what the education of our children would look like?

- ❖ Would our kids be able to go to college?

- ❖ The list goes on…

These questions were constantly swirling in our minds. Anxiety over the decision was my constant companion. While my husband and I were bold and crazy enough to think we might just be able to educate our girls ourselves and allow for flexibility and time for our girls to pursue their own unique interests, it did not come without years of consideration.

We both remember the day we withdrew the girls from the system. My husband was at work and described having a "terrible sinking feeling" – like we were making a huge mistake and tried to call me before I went, but I had already finished. I remember walking out the doors of the school terrified but exhilarated, *free*. I had no idea the journey we were about to begin. As I have said before, six years later, I

15

only wish I had done it sooner.

---

*We knew we were "good", but we
wanted "great!"*

We wanted a vibrant life!

This is not a public-school bash book. I was and am a
huge advocate for a strong public-school system. My
husband and I always felt we would volunteer and
participate in the public-school system as it's the foundation
for a stable, evolving society.

In the United States, the public-school system has
become far more than just a place for education, but for
many a place for meals, before/after school and medical
care. This is a huge demand on a system that is asked to do
much with little. It is remarkable what the school system can
accomplish!

No system is perfect. None. No public-school, private
school, charter school, magnet school or homeschool has all
the answers or runs perfectly.

If you select one system over the other, there will be
pros and cons. Because this book is meant for the family
considering homeschooling that will be my slant, my take,
for the most part.

Allow me to clarify, I do not ever, ever, ever think

homeschooling is *the* answer for everyone. Nor, is it the perfect solution – that doesn't exist. It is *one* option. One if you are still reading this, you must be at least considering for your family.

I have been astounded, yes, astounded at the number of friends and friends of friends that have called, emailed or texted me since we started homeschooling with the following lead-in... "Hey Vickie, we think we might want to homeschool. Do you have time to meet for coffee, so I can pick your brain?"

Yes! I receive that call more and more and I do believe we are at the beginning of a huge revolution to bring our kids home. I believe this dramatic increase in homeschooling is one more option families are exploring in redefining what public-education is evolving into for the 21st-century student.

We, I believe, are searching for ways to try to not only educate our children, but to course-correct some of the disconnects we are currently seeing in society.

~ CHAPTER THREE ~

HOMESCHOOLING IN THE 21ST CENTURY

ON EDUCATION:
School Principal: I'm sure your children will be very happy here"
Gomez: "If we wanted them to be happy, we would've let them stay at home."
-The Addams Family

*W*e have come through a lightning-bolt warp-speed technological tsunami. Our kids live in a different world. Period. Many public-schools and policy-makers have not even begun to catch up. While this book is not going to dive into the multifaceted issues that face our children today, I cannot skim over or gloss over the negative impacts this is having on our children. We were not prepared or equipped for the consequences of all this rapid change, and our kids are suffering.

ADHD, autoimmune disorders, food allergies, behavioral and cognitive disorders, teen depression and suicide rates are escalating at alarming rates. The data is showing up, but are we paying attention? We must stop and ask ourselves, *what is happening*? What can we do to rise and partner with our youth in a way that makes them educated, healthy, and equipped to work in the 21st century? And, most importantly, **happy**?

Growing up in the 80's I feel my generation was the last 'free' generation. Our childhood was computer-free. **COMPUTER-FREE.**

We were able to disconnect before being connected was even a thing.

My first computer was in college, in the 90's. I was a latch-key kid (anyone else?) I literally had a key to my home tied around my neck on one of those white cotton braided ribbons we used to put in our hair. Anyone remember those? The ribbon had three cotton strands woven together to make thick ribbons – think Tootie on Facts of Life. I still remember the key under my t-shirt giving me VIP entry to my home **at the age of 9.**

I was a child of divorce. Both of my parents worked full-time. No one was home, all summer, all day. Do you hear me? I was in elementary school. One of my brothers was even younger than me! I "watched" him. This scenario was common in my neighborhood.

We all knew what moms stayed home. **There were 2.** *Two* on my entire street. Chrissy and Heidi's moms stayed home. We knew it was time for lunch when their moms told us it was time for our friends to come in for food. Sometimes, they would even make my brother and I a sandwich too - best peanut butter and jelly sandwiches (without crusts) ever.

We did what we wanted all day. No supervision. No checking in. No accountability (unless something got broken.) We road bikes everywhere. No helmets. No knee pads or elbow pads. Our bikes were old, hand me downs. We never had *new* bikes, ever. We played in the street. We didn't wear shoes outside. We drank from the water hose and passed it around from person to person.

We played in the woods. **We got lost**. We went to a neighbor's houses to play. We played at peoples' houses that our parents didn't know. My parents never 'cleared' or 'set up' a playdate for us, ever.

We crossed busy streets. We rode our bikes across major train tracks, 2 miles from our house, to go to the pool in the summer. The community pool - when a pool pass was $10. We would just throw our towels around our necks and go. We wore flip flops or no shoes and rode in the street, (sometimes on sidewalks) across busy intersections.

Sunscreen? *Please...*

We would take our change, stop at the candy shop and stock up on Pixie Stix's, bubble gum and the pastel colored button candy attached to strips of miles of white paper. We had such amazing freedom.

We figured things out on our own. We became resourceful, we learned to trust ourselves. I remember creating peanut butter and jelly Saltine cracker sandwiches out of necessity when we were out of bread.

Year-round sports and activities didn't exist. We did activities through the school year and occasionally summer, city-led community centers at our local elementary schools. Summers were O.F.F. Lazy. Time-laden delicious opportunities for *nothing*.

---

*We have forgotten that doing **nothing** may be the most important **something** we do in life.*

We had land lines and paper with lines for

communication. That's it. No one knew what anyone else was doing. We played with friends within in a knocking and bike-ride distance.

We had teachers, libraries, encyclopedias, movies and TV for our education. **Google didn't exist.**

Outdated Information was written in our textbooks before they were even published. When we wrote a paper on a topic, we had to use an encyclopedia and books for research. Have I mentioned, there was no Google? Information was *not* at our fingertips. We were back in that skydiving plane I described at the beginning of the book, our toes dangling on the precipice of the computer age. We had no idea how different life would become - quickly.

Teen magazines, movies, and TV shows were our only reference point to what was in style or popular. It wasn't in our face 24/7. There was no social media displaying picture-perfect lives, image after image with your self-worth affirmed with the click of a heart or 'like'.

We couldn't see what everyone was doing and whom they were doing it with. In our school-days, a letter dropped over the person's shoulder in front of you on top of your desk, or slipped in your locker, was our 'communication.'

Our world was smaller. Our world-view was smaller. We were sort of insulated, protected. We did not have 24-hour news cycles. The news came on twice, sometimes three times a day. That was it. And, if you missed it, too bad too sad.

We were not scared. We saw the world (generally speaking) as safe. We were outside. We touched it. We played in it. We imagined. We looked our friends in the eyes. We sat in our friends' bedrooms and just talked and listened to music (on the radio or tape cassette.) We had no cell phones. Even, our cameras required processing. ***Nothing 'instant.'***

I would be lying if I didn't say I am sad my kids do not know that type of world. I also would be lying if I didn't admit there were negative sides to how we were raised, too. Personally, I see 'helicopter parenting' as almost a boomerang parenting response to the lack of involvement in many of our childhoods.

I wish our kids could taste the freedom we experienced *and* have parents who are not necessarily helicoptering, but intentional. The delicate balance of hands-on and hands-off parenting.

What our children need today as students is nothing like our childhood.

Ok, at first glance, this may feel off-topic and for some of you, I may just sound old. My intention was to write a book for someone considering homeschooling, not a personal testimony of growing up in the 80's.

But, after thinking about it, I believe getting to the "why" is an important philosophical discussion when considering homeschooling. Also, this dovetails beautifully into my next chapter - and it's a big one - your ***why.***

~ CHAPTER FOUR ~

YOUR *WHY*

"Educating the mind without educating the heart is no education at all." – Aristotle

*I*f you are in the contemplation stage of considering homeschooling, you may not have an articulate "why," yet. We didn't. We only had a feeling, a nagging poke, a whisper that we desired something else.

We are discovering our 'whys' more and more each year as we continue to homeschool.

Big changes sometimes require a leap of faith.

I have a list of books and resources that we found helpful as we began homeschooling at the end of this book. However, I must mention this book straight away. It is not only a book for someone considering homeschooling, but a book for every single parent in the U.S.A. regardless of the vehicle you choose for your child's education.

Trust me. Buy it. Reserve it at the library. Start reading it today! It was not available when I started homeschooling and is rich in wisdom and content. The book is called *"Rethinking School – How to take charge of your child's education,"* by Susan Wise Bauer. If I were going to a baby shower today, this would be my gift. To me, it is a must read for every parent.

Rethinking School will provide you with tangible, hands-on information to help you wrap your brain around the current state of the United States education system. It highlights how critical it is we help find solutions to strengthen and redesign our system. Many of these solutions are going to take decades to come to fruition and most likely, your child will have graduated out of the system by then. That's sobering. The author illuminates important aspects and considerations of educating your children from preschool to high-school.

High school - sigh... This book helped calm my fears of educating my high-school age children at home. Although I was intimidated (and still am at times!) about home educating my 10th grader, I now *love* it. *Rethinking Education* helped me put structure to her courses and create a pathway in an easy to understand language.

Also, keep your eyes out for a new release in early 2019 from Julie Bogart, *The Brave Learner: Finding Everyday Magic in Homeschool, Learning and Life.* I am confident it will empower the parent homeschooling their children in the 21st century. I know it is going to be *fabulous!* Pre-order today!

Like I have previously stated, for at least the first year we homeschooled, I didn't have an answer to the question, *"why are you homeschooling?"* And, I was asked it a lot. A LOT. I came up with a quick polite sound-bite of an answer, but it has taken me almost 5 years of

homeschooling to honestly realize our *why* started out more as a feeling or intuition. It required a leap of faith, and the whys are *always* unfolding. It is almost like our whys 'show up' retrospectively and validate our decision to pull the trigger to homeschool.

My husband and I had the brazen confidence to trust we could bring our girls home. To allow them the flexibility to pursue interest-led education and activities, family togetherness, travel, and more downtime be children. To leave a system laden with homework, checkboxes and learning to prepare for a standardized test.

We thought, rather than read about the Liberty Bell, let's go see it!

Every family will have different whys.

Quickly, without overthinking it, why did you purchase this book? Why? What are you seeking? Are you gathering information? Are you unhappy with your child's current schooling options? Does your child have special needs? Are you seeking more connection within your family? Did you always think you would homeschool? Are you happy? Is life good, but you want great? Do you wish your faith to take more of a front seat in your child's education? Do you enjoy your kids and want more time with them? Do you hate homework? Are you tired? Do

you wish to step off the hamster wheel? Do *you* like to learn? Do you think standardized testing is not the way to a child's mind? Do you see other people homeschooling and think, "*I could do that...*"

One of the joys of homeschooling is
embracing your "whys." They will contain
the things that make you and your family
happy.

Your *why*. I am not talking about the conditioning and/or conformity we have been fed for years. Perhaps, the American dream is your dream, and that is cool. But, if it isn't, and you are searching for something different - if you are looking for a way to educate, love and connect with your family in a new way, homeschooling may be an option for you! Take time to lean into what your family culture thrives upon. What lights up your family? You know what's so cool? You will get to create a homeschool that reflects your passions, interests, and dreams!

Here is a list of some of Our Whys we have realized or have become clear over the last few years:

- ❖ To remember and embrace the idea that life is short, we will work *and* play hard.

- ❖ To grow global, community-based human beings who are active in the community.

- ❖ To enjoy being together and have more time as a family while our kids are young.

- ❖ **To have flexibility.** To jump off school mandated

schedules to allow for adventure and rest.

❖ To limit the amount of precious time wasted in school, sitting in carpool, waiting for the school bus, checking forms, attending mandatory meetings, etc. **Connection requires intention, involvement and time.** Our public-school life was taking huge cash advances from our family life bank account.

❖ To avoid some of the 'socialization' we were witnessing at school.

❖ To embrace Adventure! World-schooling, hands-on, experiential learning. Travel.

❖ *To celebrate* individual *uniqueness.*

❖ To opt-out of elementary and middle school homework.

❖ To allow our children to be kids as long as possible and explore the world around them. Have a less rigid or "adult-like" schedule for our children – more time to be kids, do nothing.

❖ To adopt a culture of continual learning together.

❖ To some extent, keep them safe. Sadly, at the printing of this book, there have been over 20 mass shootings in the last school year. Bullying and teen suicide, anxiety and depression rates are at an all-time high.

❖ *To encourage our kids to pursue interest-led*

learning and activities.

❖ To impress learning shouldn't have to end or begin with a bell. It can be a life-long habit.

❖ To emphasize comprehension and intelligence are not measured by a standardized test.

❖ To opt-out of a state-determined fixed course curriculum that usually does not allow for flexibility in learning or interests.

❖ To nurture my husband and my love of learning. Secret: you get to learn amazing things, too!

❖ To create a family-shared connection and context.

❖ To foster a love of learning that will hopefully endure over time.

❖ To get our kids looking up and off devices. We wanted to try to kindle a love of outdoors and nature's cycles and rhythms.

❖ To cultivate and hopefully nurture a love of learning and encourage/support independent follow-through of their interests.

❖ To explore a healthy balance of family, alone and downtime.

❖ To promote, explore, celebrate and integrate The Arts into our life.

❖ **To integrate learning and life.**

❖ To promote healthy sleep, nutrition and rest habits that can sustain them into adulthood.

❖ To dedicate time for developing life skills – organization, time-management, meal planning, and personal accountability.

❖ To discourage learning, performing or participating for a grade or praise.

❖ To promote a more restful, peaceful, balanced home and life.

I am confident as time marches forward more whys will become apparent. I guess what I am trying to say, is spend some time thinking about why *you* are considering homeschooling - but, don't get stuck if there's no clear answer. For now, to begin, maybe a gut feeling desiring something different is all you need.

What is your reason or reasons behind wanting to make a change?

Lean into your why, but don't get hung up on it.

While we are discussing your '*why*,' let's also visit your '*how*.' For many families, homeschooling will require one parent to either come home full-time or consider part-time

34

work. I say many families because I know a number of families that continue to work full-time and homeschool their children, too.

My husband and I felt for this lifestyle to work for our family, we needed me to stay home and serve as the C.E.O. of our homeschool. We took an honest look at our lifestyle and made changes to allow me to be home without the stress of money and limited time.

This was not 'easy!' We were asking our girls to make major changes, trust us on this idea of homeschooling *and* make major changes in their lifestyle, too. We felt it was important to allow them space to express their fears, sadness, and anxiety about the future- *but only for a short period of time.* We quickly worked on refocusing and looking ahead at all the exciting opportunities that we hoped were in our future.

To allow us to homeschool with less financial pressure and long-term security some big changes were required. We sold our large suburban home, downsized and modified a property to multi-generationally live.

We chose spending our money on experience and adventure, and less on maintaining and consuming.

Do you hear what I'm saying? Homeschooling ***may*** require other significant changes. Home educating your children is not just about academics. Do you hear me? You will be changing the way your family *lives*. If you are feeling the calling, the desire to make learning a family-centered lifestyle, **you CAN do it!**

~ CHAPTER FIVE ~

FINDING MENTORS & YOUR TRIBE

"But you people do not understand me, and I am afraid you never will." – Vincent Van Gogh

*W*hen I first started homeschooling, I felt lost in every way. The only thing I had ever known about education was public school. I remember feeling so dumb when I first met or talked with other homeschool moms. They spoke using jargon foreign to me. I would come home and Google things like, "lap-books," to enroll in a crash course in homeschool lingo.

For a solid two years, I felt isolated and alone. The first year was okay because everything was so new, and I was focusing on keeping us afloat. I worked diligently to create a classroom and recreate school at home. We had calendar time, repeated the Pledge of Allegiance, we had a classroom...*my word*, I sweetly smile back on those times.

I think when transitioning from public school to homeschool, many of us naturally do this. *It's almost like a stage you must pass through to get to you – **your homeschool**.* To grow your homeschool into what your vibe and culture or homeschool legacy will become.

We had our public-school friends and life (whom we adored) and simultaneously, whenever possible, we were testing out homeschool groups and gatherings. But, never quite finding "our" people. You know what I mean? Don't get me wrong, we met great people, kind people, but mostly nonsecular homeschoolers.

Let me be clear, I have no, zero, zilch issues with this or families that homeschool for faith-based reasons. I think the nonsecular groups have done a tremendous job creating community, fellowship, and programs that reflect their values. But, this was not why we were homeschooling, and I was looking for other families with a similar vision – they were a little more difficult to find.

We tried co-ops, book clubs, Meet-ups, homeschool museum days, conferences and playdates. During this time, one thing I discovered for my family was it became too easy to "get busy" going to all these activities and lose the easier pace, freedom and flexibility of being home.

My kids are involved in extracurricular activities 4-5 times a week and that was plenty of socialization – *for the most part* (not my extroverted middle child.) After time, we did find a homeschool group we jived with. They offer many fun social activities, including teen dances, which my girls have enjoyed. Finding where you thrive is going to be critical to your growth as a home educator.

Find your vibe and you will thrive!

Social media can be a powerful source of community and connection as a homeschooler. There are many online groups to support just about every style of homeschooling. I have several 'good friends' that I have never met in person (yet) who have been a huge source of support, friendship, and inspiration.

You must keep trying, reaching out, looking and trying things out until you find your peeps. When you do, you will know. I promise they are out there and will make all the difference in your well-being as a mom and a home educator.

Somewhere in my third-ish year of homeschool, I met two mentors that changed the course of my homeschool and life. One was Julie Bogart and the other was Mary Wilson.

These two women were the vision I was waiting for. Julie, a homeschool mother of five, owns a writing business called Bravewriter. She shares a revolutionary approach to teaching writing which focuses on nurturing your child's writing voice. Julie is real. She homeschooled and graduated all five of her children. Her children have graduated from college and have/are traveling the world. She is positive and full of life and hope. Julie allowed me a glimpse into my possible future. Julie was proof it is possible to be happy, complete, connected and homeschool to college.

She was like the fairy godmother of homeschooling! Not only does Julie mentor the entire family, but her courses are amazing, too. In all my years of schooling, I never was taught an approach to writing (and living) like hers – her courses almost grow writers reversing all the processes of how I learned writing in my childhood. She gently nurtures the child's writing life by first focusing on having the family read, discuss and practice writing from diverse quality literature.

At first, her courses focus on not judging, editing or red-penning early writing, but lovingly and respectfully coaxing and nurturing the unique voice of each child. Once the child is more comfortable writing from their voice, more attention is placed on the 'clean-up' process or the mechanics of writing which are important to writing, but not writing in of itself, yes? Get it?

Find a homeschool mom a few years ahead of you for vision, confidence, and encouragement.

Julie introduced me to the style of homeschooling called Charlotte Mason (I will give a brief description of some of the more popular styles of homeschooling in a later chapter.) Having a 'style' or 'philosophy' of homeschooling will help you set a foundation and plant roots in your homeschool.

Mary Wilson, my other mentor (and dear friend) lives in my city and was a middle school math teacher. She has four kids. She and her husband always knew they would homeschool. She has unending inspiring energy and is a wealth of information. She is generous with her time and such an encourager! She always makes me believe I can do anything. She is MY momma pixie-dust!

Mary encourages homeschool moms on her blog and Instagram account @NotBefore7 – and she means it, don't bother her before 7! 😊

If possible, I would encourage you to seek out a conference for homeschoolers to immerse yourself in a weekend with other homeschool moms. You can glean valuable insight from listening to other newbie homeschoolers (make you feel 'normal') and the veterans that have been there and done it.

Out of respect for my children's privacy, what I choose to share on social media tends to highlight our better moments of homeschooling. It has been essential to find a tribe I felt safe confiding and sharing my intimate truths, struggles and worries, while parenting and homeschooling. This, in my opinion, is more important than the shiny-happy Instagram worthy images we post.

So, my tribe is small but mighty. You will have to take time and effort to seek out *your* people, but I know they are there. You will find them, and they will make all the difference in your journey.

"People fear what they do not understand." – Bruce Lee

When feeling out for your tribe, one observation I have made is moms seem to fall into one of three categories – introverts, extroverts or ambiverts. As all things are not 100%, we do seem to nuzzle up more with one of these groups.

I read somewhere that you can figure out which group you most belong to by answering the following question, *"how do you recharge?"* You know what I mean? When you are looking to recharge yourself, do you seek to be with others (extrovert) or alone (introvert)? Or, perhaps a little of both (ambivert)?

I mention this because I think it's important you know yourself and honor your needs. This is essential not just if you homeschool (although this is so important when you are with your children *all the time*) but in life, too. I have a chapter later we will explore and discuss the importance of Self-Care.

I am an introvert, hands down. I love people and being with friends and family, but I recharge alone, in silence. I am one of those people that could go away for a long time, by myself, and not speak a word for days.

My husband, on the other hand, is an extrovert-squared. He lights up and thrives with people. If he is wanting to recharge, he wants to "do something" - **with people**. We could not be more polar-opposite. But, that is the beauty of knowing yourself. He honors my needs and I honor his. We both recharge the way we need, and this allows us to bring our best selves to the table and our family almost every day.

Family. When finding your tribe, you may find you have to distance yourself and not share everything with some friends and sadly, sometimes your own family. It's ok. Truly, it is.

Family can be our greatest source of strength and sometimes our worst source of frustration or sabotage. I have heard many stories of families expressing nothing but negative or anxious thoughts about a family's decision to homeschool. If you need, for now, don't play the sharing game. Have some quick, close-ended responses and then perform what I call "the pivot" until you feel more confident. Here is an example:

> Mom: *"What are you going to do about socialization, honey? You don't want your kids to be weird, do you?"*
>
> You: *"Mom, I hear you. We have concerns about that, too but trust this is the best decision for our family right now –* **and pivot** *- Hey, I really want to hear about what's going on with you! How was your trip? Tell me all about it!"*

You don't have to defend your choices. There is nothing to prove. Talk with people that are legit interested in your journey and work on a few 'one-liners' for the rest. You will feel much better while you are finding your footing and building your confidence.

I remember one time a dear friend of mine shared that her sister-in-law (someone I have met *once*) told her **she** worried about our decision to homeschool. In particular, **she** had concerns about our oldest, that she might be missing out on opportunities by being home. I had to laugh! I told my friend, "Tell you sister-in-law thanks for her concern (insert snark) because I didn't already have enough concern *all on my own!*"

You must realize that a choice to homeschool inherently juxtaposes their choice, it just does. You are choosing to leave a system they are staying in. To some, not all, that can be unsettling.

"Most people do not listen with the intent to understand; they listen with the intent to reply." -Steven Covey

---

Lastly, I am not saying your spouse must support the decision to homeschool 100%, but boy I hope he or she is in your tribe. While you can isolate yourself from some family and friends at this early kind of vulnerable stage, your spouse like lives with you.

It has been my experience that the primary caregiver is the one that does all the reading, discussing and thinking about a decision to homeschool. They then kind of brief the other parent on the information. In this phase of considering homeschooling, make sure you are keeping them in the loop.

If possible, consider having your spouse meet with other spouses of homeschoolers. It can be helpful for them to hear others experiences of bringing their children home. Sometimes their concerns may surprise you. For example, my husband was on board with homeschooling, far before me. However, when we got ready to dive in, his biggest concern? Money!

We had always planned on me returning to nursing as the kids became older. My hubby owns his own business and he had anxiety about realizing he was going to be totally responsible for all our finances - I think it felt daunting. *Listen* to your partner's concerns and thoughts. You don't always have to agree, but you must be able to hold space to hear what is in each of your hearts and minds.

I have friends whose partners were not on board at the beginning and how they handled it was an awesome compromise. They agreed to "try it out," not to commit to homeschooling for the long haul, but to just be open to giving it a try. Honestly, I would say you have to at least give it a few years to let the dust settle and find your stride, but it is a starting point. Once you begin, your spouse will start to see the changes in your home and may come around.

Your tribe consists of friends, family, and your community. When you shift into homeschooling plan on feeling a little shake-up and shake-down of your circles. It's ok to allow some friends and family to drift outside the circle for a period of time while you are working on redefining and reconfiguring your life. There is no exact blueprint for you, which is exciting and scary at times.

Many of your friends and family have stayed in the 'known,' - the familiar. If you removed your children from public school, you are leaving an entrenched system for something new, foreign. Many of your friends, with good intentions, are going to make you doubt your decision.

I am just recommending, in the beginning, when you are on unstable ground, surround yourself with only people that raise your vibration, encourage you and have your back. Be cautious whom you share your story with and how much, at least until you have some experience and have strengthened your muscle of confidence. *This is true for most things in life, not just homeschooling.*

~CHAPTER SIX~

STYLES OF HOMESCHOOLING

"Education is an atmosphere." – Charlotte Mason

*N*o matter how you slice it, finding your philosophy or own family-culture of home education will help you create the masterpiece of a life you desire. Like Michelangelo believed he just needed to chip away the marble to create his masterpieces, you too will do the work to manifest your unique homeschool and life. There are a plethora of styles and ways of homeschooling out in the big beautiful world - too many to list or describe completely. I will highlight a few of the more popular styles to give you a taste or a palette of styles to consider.

Please note these are just general descriptions. My goal is to expose you to some of the styles of homeschooling and if one sounds more like your personality, you can do further investigation. I would encourage you to search out Facebook groups, Meet-up groups, and other venues to learn more.

I promise no homeschool looks like another. Just because one method may say to do x, y or z, it doesn't mean you *have* to. Many homeschools I know are a blending of many styles and philosophies, *especially* when you have multiple children.

Finding a style or vibe of homeschooling is like finding the *setting* for your tribe. It may take time for you to find what feels good to you and it is not uncommon for it to change through the years or even seasons!

You may have to homeschool for a little while until you are clear on your strengths and your own personal mom/family preferences. For example, if you hate nature and being outside, homeschooling in the Charlotte Mason style (where outdoor play and nature are essential) may not be the best fit for your family, but pieces of her philosophy may still resonate.

Below is an introduction to the eight most common styles of homeschooling.

> **Charlotte Mason** – Charlotte Mason was an early 1900's educator in England. Her methods are a popular style of homeschooling. One of her famous mantras, *"Education is an atmosphere, a discipline, a life,"* directly points to how homeschooling is a *lifestyle* not 'school' at home.

Her methods are widely used in homeschools across the globe. Our family uses a modified Charlotte Mason method. I blend (like many) Charlotte Mason, unschooling and the Bravewriter Lifestyle to form an eclectic homeschool. Charlotte Mason believed children were born whole and are not to be 'fed' information.

She goes further to suggest children are born complete and whole and our job is to nourish and support their unique gifts and talents as they grow.

Outdoor play and nature studies are an essential element of this method of homeschooling. Quality literature copy work and dictation are fundamental tools to her style of education, too. Charlotte Mason allows children a lot of time to explore and integrate the world around them.

➤ **Unschooling** – Don't let the name kid you, unschooling is not "no schooling." Unschooling is child-led, interest-based learning. Learning appears to happen more naturally and, in many ways, how we prefer to learn as adults.

Unschooling doesn't focus on benchmarks or timetables but allows the child to take the lead on learning by expressing interest in topics or subjects. This type of homeschooling honors the idea that children are naturally curious and will learn, period.

Your role is to listen and support their interests as they present with immersion and exposure to information. Unschoolers, generally are out and about in their community and seem to follow a looser schedule.

➤ **Classical** – This method of homeschooling has been around for a long time. I believe since the 1400-1500's! Classical Education encourages children to learn for themselves using a very specific formula and guidelines. Classical homeschool families typically have a structured day that allows for a balance of academia, worship, chores and family time.

In Classical Education, history is an important subject and is taught in a unique way that other styles of homeschoolers sometimes borrow to use for themselves. Classical educators consider this type of education being "complete."

➢ **School-at-home** – This type of home education is a very popular choice when families are just starting out, especially families that have never or didn't think they would be homeschooling. Why? Because it is basically trying to re-create public school at home.

The curriculum is usually boxed-set or prepackaged, and children rotate and complete tasks similar to public school. Many families realize, all on their own, after the first year that this is not ideal (for most.)

Homeschool is not public school. Homeschool is HOMEschooling, not public school at home. Learning at home is unique because you can incorporate the principles of home to school. Many times, people will leave or adapt this style of learning to reflect the flexibility and more 'fun' interest-based type of learning where the parent pulls in materials to teach their children.

A school-at-home family usually has a rigid schedule (note, not a routine) and it has been suggested, the highest level of burn out (if maintained for a lengthy amount of time.)

➢ **Waldorf** – Waldorf education was created by Rudolf Steiner. This method of education embraces the concept of educating the whole child – their heart, mind, body, and spirit.

The Arts and minimal technology are encouraged. A Waldorf home will have more of a routine (things happen in a certain order from day to day) instead of a strict schedule. Children are not only educated in subjects but encouraged to participate in the running of the home and playing outdoors.

- ➤ **Montessori** – Maria Tecla Artemisia Montessori (whew!) created the Montessori Method used in many public, private and homeschools in the early 1900's. Maria was a physician and educator and was a single mother, too!

There are many Montessori based preschools and elementary schools in the USA and is a popular choice among homeschoolers. The Montessori method allows as much unstructured time for children as possible.

Montessori recommends high-quality toys and educational material be organized attractively and available over busy, cluttered environments. It seems families that embrace a minimalist type of lifestyle would find this method enticing.

It is common for multiple ages to be learning side-by-side in this method. Instead of rotating 'subjects' you may see more center-typed learning areas set up and the child chooses what and when they wish to learn that particular subject.

- ➤ **Bravewriter Lifestyle** – While you may not find this

listed as a method of homeschooling (yet) this style of homeschooling has a growing and enthusiastic base. The creator, Julie Bogart supports growing writers and encourages connection in the home.

Bravewriter is an online writing program. Writing is taught in a revolutionary way that encourages children and the parents to find and write using their own unique voice.

Bravewriter uses language-rich, quality literature to bring families together. Julie has blended many Charlotte Mason ideas (copy work, dictation, read aloud) and brought it to the 21st century.

Her online writing classes offer a pioneering and creative approach to the writing process. She not only mentors families in writing, but she supports the well-being of the entire homeschool family.

She homeschooled five children of her own and has the unique perspective to share with the homeschool community. All five of her kids have graduated from high school and have successfully launched into the world. She gives inspiration and never denies or sugar-coats the reality of the task of homeschooling.

Julie stresses routine over schedule (but really, she reinforces whatever works for *your* family as most important.)

Bravewriter uses tools like Poetry Tea Time, Freewrite Fridays and family read aloud as anchors of the homeschool. My family is a Bravewriter Family.

➢ **Relaxed/Eclectic** – I believe many families fall somewhere into this category. Even if you lean or heavily sit in one method, it is very common to see families pull in ideas or concepts from other methods they enjoy. You may find one of your children thrive in the school-at-home method and your other child learns best as an unschooler. Or, you may find you like elements of all methods and create your own method! I truly believe the eclectic type of schooling allows for more freedom, flexibility, creativity, and joy in the home.

~ CHAPTER SEVEN ~

SCHEDULE vs. ROUTINE

At first, they'll ask you why you're doing it.

Later, they'll ask you how you did it.

-unknown

hen considering homeschooling take some time to ponder if you and your family are more schedule or routine based.

Not sure the difference? Let me try to demonstrate - my family is more routine – based. We find a 'schedule' stressful and counter-intuitive to how we like to learn as a family. When we are doing our read aloud, if we come across a concept, idea, word, time-period, or geographical location being on a routine *allows us time* to go down the rabbit hole without fear of *'getting behind.'*

Perhaps the best way is to illustrate the difference. Here is a typical day for us when we are home *and* schooling.

For me, public school has a schedule. Start/Stop times, little flexibility or wiggle room *for life*. A routine, which provides a structure with flexibility, seems to vibe with being home better. (I know not for everyone.)

- **6am-8 am-ish** I wake up before everyone to have me-time, quiet reflection, coffee, morning walk and dress for the day.

- **6:30 am-ish** my high schooler wakes up and does her math independently, leaves for me to review and she works out.

- **7 am-ish** my middle and youngest wake-up and make their breakfast, have some morning technology time, clean-up, math, copywork and are ready for

58

9amish read-aloud.

- **9 am-ish** Monday Morning Meeting (if it's a Monday.) We meet with our calendars and review the week, add anything significant to calendars and discuss what's coming up. We touch in and see how everyone is and lay the foundation for the week.

I try to set the breakfast table with something special - flowers from outside, a candle, yummy treats, special cups to spread a little "pixie dust" when possible.

After our Monday meeting, or if it is not a Monday, we go to the living room or outside if nice for Read Aloud.

- **9 am-11 am-ish** Read Aloud. This is the foundation of our homeschool.

Now that my eldest is in high school she doesn't always stay for the entire read aloud. She has more ownership over her time now as she works more independently on her high school studies.

We also use this time for group learning. Generally, I do history, geography, grammar and special subjects together. I rotate subjects.

- **11 am-ish** Lunch

- **11:30 am-ish** Independent work or any deep dives or special projects.

For example, last week we did an online art course and spent an hour or so each day completing various art projects.

- **1 pm-ish** Is our goal 'end' time and girls then have free time. I encourage them to go outside as much as possible.

Typically, our girls have activities in evening and dinner time varies based on activities. We strive to have dinner as a family, as much as possible, every evening – even it that means it is 8pm.

Our routine has some regular activities we look forward to like Poetry Tea Time Tuesday (which sometimes occurs on a Wednesday!) and Freewrite Fridays.

- **9:00-10 pm-ish** Bedtime.

The 'ish' connotes *flexibility*. If it is a day we have decided to take off for adventure, go to a museum, play outdoors, go on vacation, we skip our home routine and learn on the road!

If we have had a late night the evening before, we can sleep in and shift the schedule forward a couple hours, *it is flexible.*

Schedules have specific start and end times and typically rotates subjects consistently. Schedules, in my opinion, are great for some personalities but for some can create stress and a feeling of 'getting behind.'

A routine seems like a gentler way to schedule your life. Remember, you are at home, you aren't at a public school where a bell rings, you clean up and move on.

Your home has properties that the public school does not. It's more relaxed, cozy, organic. There are no bells marking the end of a period and this allows freedom to linger with a conversation or material if desired. My favorite homeschooling days are when we read aloud or when a lesson triggers a deep dive into a topic and/or opens a discussion on a meaningful level.

Another aspect of learning at home is you are constantly creating a shared narrative and/or context between subjects and family members. I can not even count the number of times we all recognize connections in time periods, events or aspects across the curriculum.

For example, this year in our history (which I do with all grade levels combined) we studied the Medieval Time Period. Our history was better understood by learning about European geography and how topography influences civilization organization and wars.

In our literature, we read a historical fiction book called *The Inquisitor's Tale*. This story took my two youngest on a Medieval adventure and solidified many of the ideas we learned in our history curriculum.

Remember how I said we wanted the flexibility to travel and learn *in* the world? We were able to layer all this with a trip to England and France at the end of the school year. Our girls touched, tasted, smelled and look at Medieval history - palaces, museums, castles, and even the London Tower!

Because we did this together, we have a shared understanding and narrative of this time period. We can, and do, reminisce. I believe they integrate what they have learned at a much deeper, tangible level...not just for a test and then forgotten by most...do you see the difference?

When the classroom size is smaller, your children are given the chance to share what *they* are *thinking*. Your children will have a much better chance to have *their* voice, *their* take on what they are learning heard.

You get the gift of hearing your child's interior landscape – their thoughts and unique viewpoints on the world and validate their importance. *That's powerful*.

~ CHAPTER EIGHT ~

Momma Self-Care

"Beautiful girl, take care of yourself. No one else knows what your soul needs."
        @random-and-lauren IG account

otherhood isn't for wimps, right? Well, sister, homeschooling is like motherhood on steroids. What I mean by that, is if you are homeschooling your children, you will be with your children in your home- 24/7.

No matter how supportive or involved of a spouse you may have, much of the logistics and handling of homeschooling will fall upon your shoulders and weigh upon your heart in a way many will never understand.

When I worked outside my home, I had to balance my home and professional life. I did get time apart from my children. I talked to adults and interacted in the adult world.

When you homeschool, your kids are with you constantly. Even if they are taking classes elsewhere you are still driving, supervising and together. I cannot emphasize this point enough.

Taking good care of yourself will be paramount to a creating a home of peace, love and low stress. Will it be perfect? Will you never be frustrated, tired, overwhelmed? Nope. But, with intentional design and awareness, you can put into place healthy self-care rituals and practices that will ground you and keep you balanced as you educate and share your days together at home. This is not only beneficial for you, but what great role modeling for your children about taking care of yourself.

Do a personal inventory of yourself. Are you struggling

with something big? I am talking about depression, illness, your marriage is crumbling, family crisis, severe financial instability... you must handle these before setting out to educate your children at home.

Perhaps you need to handle some situations or do some personal work before bringing your kids home. Like Charlotte Mason so beautifully stated, *"Education is an atmosphere..."*

You must look at what you're bringing your children home to, is it healthy? Are you ok?

I am **not** implying you cannot navigate any of the above-mentioned situations *while* homeschooling, but what I *am* encouraging is you must be taking the steps (therapy, counseling, coaching, etc.) to help you learn and grow into the best version of yourself. You and your kids deserve it.

I believe if you do this honestly and openly with your children (as appropriate) it could be a far more valuable, real-life educational experience than any academic lesson you could possibly create.

Once you have done a personal inventory and feel ready to homeschool, *'momma self-care'* is

essential-whatever that looks like for you.

Every mother has their 'done,' 'stick-a-fork-in-me,' done.

The goal is to try to become aware of the signs and symptoms **before** you are done. To do the self-care needed to maintain a healthy, happy mom.

As I stated earlier, I am an introvert. I know if I go too long without a day alone, in silence, or we get too busy *doing* and not *being,* I get irritable and that never translates well to homeschooling.

I try hard to honor my needs by taking time alone each morning. Every few months my husband and I arrange a weekend that he takes the girls on an adventure, so I can have a long weekend alone.

I also have learned to say *"no"* for self-care. I realized when weekends came many of my friends and family were always trying to arrange activities and get-togethers. I get it. They worked all week; their kids were in school all week and they want to play and connect. However, for me, at this phase of life, I need the weekends to unplug and recharge.

Self-care is not a luxury it is a necessity.

~ CHAPTER NINE ~

RULES & REGULATIONS

"There are no educational emergencies."
-Stephanie Elms

ach state will have their own rules and regulations for homeschooling. You will need to visit your state's department of education website for the specifics and qualifications to homeschool.

Some states are easier to homeschool in than others. For example, some states require learning portfolios and supervision visits from the states to operate a homeschool. While others have less oversight or regulations.

In my state, North Carolina, a home educator is required to have a high school diploma. We are required to register our homeschool (you do once) and then annually keep an immunization and attendance record for each child. Annually, children are required to have some form of a standardized test administered either at a testing facility or by the home educator (submitting results is optional.) *That's it!*

I remember the day I took my kids out of public school. All I had to do was complete an easy form indicating my intent to withdrawal and turn it into the school. That was it. Five years later, my only regret?

I wish I had done it sooner.

Finally, just a little suggestion on naming your homeschool. When naming your homeschool, think long-term and not 'cute.' If your child decides to go to college "Takei Academy" sounds much more impressive than "The

Sunshine and Happiness Homeschool."

~CHAPTER TEN ~

CURRICULUM

"When the tears begin the learning ends. "
-Julie Bogart

*T*here are literally a million different homeschool curriculum options at your fingertips -from prepackaged expensive box curriculum to online courses to free curriculum downloadable from the Internet.

Once again, this is just my opinion, but I would suggest you buy very little curriculum at one time. I remember the summer before we started our first year of homeschooling. I spent weeks looking online and spending a bundle on curriculum for my rising 1st, 3rd and 5th grader.

Perhaps it is just a natural stage of a homeschooler one must do, but now I say it is so not needed! But, I have been there, and you must do what makes *you* feel confident and prepared as you begin your marathon called homeschooling. Remember, this is not a sprint! You are in it for the long haul, baby!

Only purchase curriculum you need
for that semester.

One way to quickly overwhelm yourself, your space and make you feel like you are behind is to have shelves and piles and cabinets full of unused (and usually expensive) curriculum. If you do end up purchasing curriculum and supplies for the entire year, the future or plan on keeping some material for other children in your home as they age-up, consider putting it away – *out of sight* until needed.

The success of your homeschool is not about the curriculum, don't overthink it.

If you have a preschooler, do not buy curriculum. (Unless you just cannot help yourself!) Just read, read, read and play outdoors! Seriously.

Before you purchase any curriculum take time to get clear on what it is you wish to accomplish with your children for the semester. Be realistic!

I highly recommend purchasing the book "Minimalist Homeschooling" by Zara Fagen to help you get clear on your goals and set realistic expectations and goals for your year/semester. This book was a game changer for me.

If Minimalism isn't your thing, don't let the name scare or turn you off. The premise of Minimalist Homeschooling is spending your time learning what you need/love and cutting out anything unnecessary or distracting you from your homeschooling goals.

The author provides worksheets that help you refine and define your vision, goals, and principles of your homeschool. Once you have done that, purchasing or collecting curriculum becomes easier and there is less waste of money and physical and mental space!

Once you decide on your subjects you wish to cover, see if the library contains any of your books and reserve. Next, check out and see if you have a local homeschool store that sells on consignment. This can save you a ton of money!

I used to pay full price for my math curriculum until a friend told me about our local homeschool consignment store. Now, I sell our old curriculum and purchase used textbooks, too! Plus, it is fun to check out all the curriculum available. I allowed my high schooler to select her history curriculum and she thought that was cool.

As you make choices in curriculum consider your child's learning styles and preferences. Decide whether you wish your curriculum to be secular (nonreligious) or nonsecular (religious). Take some time to visit blogs of homeschoolers you feel embody your vibe and see what they are using. Many times, they will do a product review and give their feedback and give you real, hands-on feedback of the curriculum.

A curriculum is just a tool. I have found that less is better - always. The curriculum is no exception. A healthy home environment with an engaged mother who has curiosity will trump curriculum evertime.

~ CHAPTER ELEVEN ~

TIPS WHILE TRANSITIONING

"There is no single effort more radical in its potential for saving the world than a transformation of the way we raise our children. "

-   Marianne Williamson

*T*ips as you begin:

If you are anything like me, at first, seeing my social media feed fill with the cutest pictures of my public-school friends 1st days and last days of school, homecoming games, proms and dances filled me with anxiety that *my children were missing out.* Total #FOMO. Now, I see it as #JOMO – joy of missing out!

Know what I did? ***Stop looking***! Consider staying away from social media on the first day of school, last days of school, proms and other 'triggers' that make you doubt your decision...it's easy to allow those few snapshots of school make you doubt your entire big picture.

Eventually, as my confidence grew, I begin posting our first day of school pictures, too. 😌

Insulate yourself and protect yourself from the questioning or the doubters. You will have enough doubt yourself and the last thing you need is a cackle of public-school moms adding to your insecurities.

Remember: people defend what they wish to protect.

You are stepping out of the story, the common narrative, you are *choosing differently*. People will naturally want to protect, defend and justify their choices. It's crazy, but it's true. We all do it.

I have discovered that as you begin, the disorientation and untethering I felt for the first couple years is to be expected. This unmooring is not only normal, but I would say essential to self-discovery and the evolution of your family. I know it's not comfortable, but change is not meant to be.

Many veteran homeschool parents even encourage some families starting homeschooling to spend time *deschooling*. Deschooling is not only **not** doing school but allowing time for the child (and family) to step away from education. To allow time for the family to decompress, relax and sometimes allow the child to begin repairing, if needed, their academic self- confidence.

Take care of yourself, momma. Practice good self-care, especially now. Find a wise person, ahead of you that can serve as a light of hope. A beacon.

Trust yourself.

Trust the process.

It works.

Love your kids, your home, and your family fiercely.

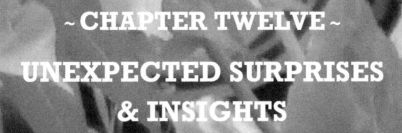

~ CHAPTER TWELVE ~
UNEXPECTED SURPRISES & INSIGHTS

"When a flower doesn't bloom,

you fix the environment in which it grows.

Not the flower."

– Alexander Den Heijer

*N*o doubt if you choose homeschooling, you will discover and find things you hadn't anticipated or planned. Here are some of my surprises, in no particular order or significance.

Things always take longer than you expect. This is true in life and homeschooling is no different. To really enjoy the freedom homeschooling allows, go for quality over quantity. Leaving space or margin in your day will make for a more satisfying homeschool experience.

Last year, I read and adopted many principles outlined in a book called *Minimalist Homeschooling.* The strategies in the book helped me realistically set up a plan for our school year that did not overwhelm, but we enjoyed.

In *Minimalist Homeschooling,* the author outlines how to determine main courses of study and strategies to help you remained focused. For example, each semester I now only keep items on my shelves and read aloud basket we are using for that six-week term. I try not to purchase curriculum until needed and consign items immediately when we are done. Any future curriculum for the year is contained in one plastic tub I keep stored out of sight until needed.

For me, this makes a huge difference in staying focused on what we are learning presently and not subconsciously making me feel overwhelmed.

Being the cafeteria lady is no joke. Depending on the ages of your children, meal preparation, serving and clean-up can take a solid 2 hours a day! If you have a four to five-hour school day - **two hours is significant**. My recommendation would be to find ways that support you in the kitchen. For me, meal planning and empowering your kids in the kitchen can be life savers.

I found when my children were younger, meal times were simpler because their routines were easier – standardized – bedtimes and wake up times were more uniform. As our girls became tweens and now teens, each girl has unique activities, preferences and sleep/wake schedules. Other than lunch, I do not have set meal times. I have a meal plan, but there is a day to day flow to the timing.

To roll with the flexibility of homeschooling and partner with natural teen sleep-wake schedules I only make breakfast for everyone once a week! Every Monday, our homeschool starts the week with our Monday Morning Meeting, a.k.a. "MMM." I go all out and create a huge breakfast, set our dining room table with candles and special items.

Our MMM has become an anchor of our homeschool. We kick-off the school week with a special breakfast, reminisce about things that happened over the week/weekend and each girl brings their calendar to our gathering to look at the week ahead. It is time to set our intentions and discuss the plans for the week over a warm breakfast. I have found sitting with the girls and reviewing the week ahead also allows them to better understand the context of our life for the next five days. The meeting assists them in planning their time accordingly.

The rest of the week, the girls are on their own for breakfast. They are more than capable to make and clean-up their own breakfast. I promise the weeks I take the time to meal plan up front, go smoother than weeks I do not.

Planning, prepping and enjoying lunch together is a priority for me. I am trying to teach our girls that meals are a time for connection, enjoyment and eating nutritious food (most of the time.) I hope they see the value in not eating their meals on the run, but as a part of taking care of their bodies and taking a break from their daily activities of life.

I keep a large Post-It note grocery list near our refrigerator with a pen underneath. In our family, everyone has developed the habit of adding things to this list as we run low or if they have a special request. When it is time for me to shop, I just snag the Post-It note and slap up a new one. For you techno-savvy mothers, I have heard there are apps for family grocery shopping lists and there are even grocery delivery services available to you as well!

I keep my refrigerator cleaned out as much as possible by tossing leftovers at the end of each week. Our refrigerator has unspoken 'zones' that items are kept for easy inventory. Each week, before I meal plan, I take a good look at what is left in our pantry, freezer, and fridge to take into consideration the meals ahead.

Immediately after grocery shopping, I try to prep lunches

and dinners as much as possible. I wash, rinse, cut, chop fruits and vegetables and place in containers straight away. I have found having your meal plan posted with as much prep work completed beforehand adds a degree of ease to your homeschool day. The upfront planning can help eliminate the extra energy required to try to create meals on the spot.

Include all family members in chores and activities of the house as soon as possible. Seriously. One sure way to Momma Burn-Out is to try to do everything yourself! You will be surprised at what your children are capable of.

Teach your children to care for themselves and be a member of a family by enlisting their assistance from as early as they can put a toy away. Cultivating a sense of ownership in their ability to wake-up, clean their bathrooms, prepare meals and do their laundry will create capable adults and spread the workload over the house to make sure you, the mother, has time to rest and participates in life-giving activities for yourself.

This does not happen with the snap of your fingers. At first, it will require time, patience, creativity and partnership while they are learning how to cook their breakfast, do their laundry or clean a bathroom. You will have to work alongside them, mentor them, not be hypercritical of the outcome and praise the effort. One day, you will be delighted when they handle it on their own – they can do it! *Let them*!

You do not need a school room in your home. I repeat,

you do not *need* a school room in your home. If you have the space and desire to do so, great, go for it! But, I have found many times, in many homes, much homeschooling tends to occur around the kitchen table and in a common living area, like the living room.

Our first year I converted our bonus room into a school room and while I loved the way it looked, I found we spent little time learning in it. To learn, I discovered we tended to gather in more common areas, centrally located and more comfortable. We no longer have a school room and I keep our homeschooling supplies and materials in one small area of my kitchen in an attractive cabinet. Homeschooling in common areas seems to flow more naturally than in a separate room isolated from the heart of our home. I have a rolling supply cart, printer, and a desk right in my kitchen – a place I find myself a lot.

Housecleaning. I wish I was someone who didn't have to have a clean home or could live in a little mess/chaos, but I am not. At first, aside from meal planning, keeping our house clean was a constant source of irritation for me. As a newbie, I found homeschooling such an enormous time commitment physically and mentally that the last thing I wanted to do in the evening or weekend was clean!

I would apply the same advice as I shared with meal preparation and enlist your family early on in helping keep your home clean.

Depending on your need for clean and your unique financial situation, I found the following two strategies extremely helpful in supporting me as a stay-at-home mom and home-educator.

When my children were younger and I was a new home educator, I found cleaning my home a source of irritation and found myself building resentment. Remember the chapter I discussed taking care of yourself? I knew I was burning out because I was not honoring my own needs and felt like I was always doing for others with little time to do the things I enjoyed. This is not a luxury. Time for yourself is not a 'nice thing,' it must be a priority and you can find creative ways to make it happen!

After talking with my husband, we agreed to two things to support me at home. We hired an affordable housekeeper who came every other week to clean our home. I called her Saint Maria and she was a gift from above. Saint Maria supported me for a year. During that year, I focused on refining my skills as a home educator and diligently worked on our second agreement – simplifying or minimalizing all areas of our home and life.

Minimalizing our home ended up being about a two-year process and honestly never ends. By removing excess things from our space, we saved time needed for cleaning, organizing and looking for items.

Most importantly, for me, it frees up mental energy. Once you remove extra physical items from your life, you naturally may find yourself wanting to clean up mental, spiritual and family scheduling as well.

So, perhaps hiring help isn't an option for you, there are still strategies you can explore to support you as the C.E.O. of your home to honor time for yourself and for rest.

Each season of life presents with new delights and challenges and having systems in place that almost run on autopilot can support you as you navigate the new territory.

Learning in your 30s and 40's rocks! Homeschooling your children is not just for them! Want to hear one of the coolest benefits of homeschooling? *You learn too!* Now that you have had some life and experience under your belt, circling back to math, history, and other subjects allows you to see things different - contextually. I now see history not as a 'subject,' but a story...a long, rich, complicated evolution of our human story.

I have developed a love of Shakespeare that I can *promise* you I never would have developed if it were not for home educating my oldest daughter. When your children are given opportunities to pursue interest-based learning, many times they will deep dive into material and take you on the adventure with them! Seriously, Hamlet might be the most brilliant relevant play ever written, just sayin'.

Your first step in the opposite flow of society is the most unsettling. I feel like this statement has been a major theme in this book. I know this book is for those considering homeschooling, but I would say it applies to anything you hear whispering in your ear that scares you a little to try.

Homeschooling is like a gateway drug **to** <u>you</u>. Does that make sense?

I have found that it is at the time you reverse your thoughts, challenge your being or take the road less traveled you find more of whom you were meant to be.

Swimming upstream requires a new set of muscles - muscles that will grow as you use them more regularly. I would equate swimming upstream as finding your way in life. It's an opportunity to become clear on who and what you believe and then trusting yourself to begin exercising that muscle of being you.

It becomes easier and easier and almost fun to start asking "why" to anything you are told you are "supposed to do." And, hear me, this is coming from a rule follower! This is *your* life, *your* family, **you** get to decide.

Less is more. Less is more. Less is more. Once again, this motto is true in life *and* homeschooling. Time is a precious resource not to be wasted. By clarifying your *why*, values and priorities, you can streamline your focus to make space for the things that matter to you.

Take the time to question how you are doing life. Ask yourself, your partner and family, *"Are we living our best life? Is the way we live In alignment with our values? Are we truly deeply happy?"* Be truthful with yourself. Do the work to clarify you and your family's vision, purpose, and values. There are many books and resources available to assist you on that journey. Once clear, it will become easier for you to release activities, subjects, expectations, and people that no longer support your life. By releasing the excess, you will have time to focus on what matters.

I would recommend doing this work regardless of how your children are educated to live a more peaceful, restful and meaningful life that resonates in your heart. *Your life, your heart...*

I hope this collection of thoughts may help you as your contemplating your decision to possibly homeschool or make a major change in your life. Regardless of your decision, your children are going to be awesome! You know how I know? Because you are reading this which means you are invested in doing good by your child.

Your kids will be awesome.

Go forward and create the family and home **you** desire based on your family culture, your strengths, and talents. Enjoy your family. Let your life be your legacy! **Rock on, friend.**

Living our Adventure!

Let's Connect!

Vickie Takei
Email: qvtakei@yahoo.com
Much neglected blog: rockonliving.com
Instagram: @rockonliving
Facebook: Rockonliving – Homeschool

If I could send you a gift basket with the books I would recommend reading regarding your decision to homeschool, these would be the ones!

A Gracious Space – Spring, Fall & Winter Editions by Julie Bogart (daily inspirational messages for the homeschool momma)

Becoming Barenaked by Jenn Barenaked

Creative Schools – The Grassroots Revolution that's Transforming Education by Ken Robinson, Ph.D.

Last Child in the Woods – Saving our Children from Nature-Deficit Disorder by Richard Louv

Minimalist Homeschooling – A Values-Based Approach to Maximize Learning and Minimize Stress by Zara Fagen, Ph.D.

Rethinking School – How to Take Charge of Your Child's Education by Susan Wise Bauer (this book is spectacular for every single parent, regardless of educational route)

The Conscious Parent by Shefali Tsary, Ph.D.

The End.

"I have this blank canvas in front of me, which is what my life can be." -Lea Michele

I'm Vickie. I am just shy of 50 years old and a retired critical care nurse. Quinn and I have been married for 23 years, together for 30! We have three daughters, Kayah (16), Kira (14) and Kamiko (11). We currently live in Raleigh, North Carolina and are in our 6th year of homeschooling! I love to travel, journal, read, wine, The Arts, and thunderstorms. My vice? Doughnuts. I love a good doughnut.

One of my self-care rituals I do almost every day is to take morning walks before life wakes up. I look for something new in nature every single day that delights my spirit. I share these observations on my IG feed daily as my **"Morning Walk Delight."** All the images in this book are snaps from some of my walks. I savor the time alone, outside in nature nurturing the practice of observation.

I feel in my heart we are on the crest of a new wave of how and what homeschooling can look like and am *so* excited to be part of the movement.

Cheers, friends! Rock on, LIVING!
Vickie

Made in the USA
Las Vegas, NV
26 May 2021